The Zen C

ISBN: 1456451723
EAN-13: 9781456451721

PRINTED IN THE UNITED STATES OF AMERICA

Contents

Chapter 1
Why Enlightened Dog Training?

Zen - a major school of Buddhism that emphasizes enlightenment through meditation & insight
Chien — French for dog

Enlightened means rational, well-informed and free of ignorance or prejudice. What does that have to do with dog training? There is a lot of conflicting information out there as to the fanciest, easiest, glitziest, oldest, newest way to train your dog. It can be overwhelming and confusing to most dog owners. This book is intended to help you cut through all the marketing and hype to get to the information to help *you* teach *your* dog.

I don't care about celebrities' dogs; I care about your dog. I don't care about the latest TV show about training, I care about what works. My approach is to use scientific learning theory and a Zen concept of working with natural ideas instead of against them to teach dogs how to behave appropriately.

Enlightenment is about awakening. Awakening the knowledge and the understanding to teach dogs appropriately. The result is a dog that is not just o.k., but one that is, well - fabulous.
Scientific learning theory includes such things as; classical conditioning, operant conditioning, conditioned reinforcers and so forth. I won't bore you with why things work (there's thousands of other books out there for that), I just want to share with you as easily and simply as I can the things that do work. How to teach your dog how they should behave when they live with us and to have a little fun while doing it is the point of this book.

The first objective is simple - *harm none*. Sometimes we can actually make behaviors worse by inadvertently rewarding behaviors we don't want, we'll talk about that at length later. The biggest mistake we can make, however, is using punishment wrong. Punishment *is* powerful, that is why if you don't understand what you are doing you can easily send your dog the wrong message. In times of stress, like when you find your brand new pair of Nike's shredded or poop behind the sofa for the millionth time, breathe deep and remember, "Harm none."

I have such immense respect and admiration for dogs the last thing I want to do is harm them. Of course, I'm a huge animal lover and have been lucky enough to work and live with a variety of species. Training a pot belly pit to stay, a cat to come or a cockatiel to fetch is just as much fun as teaching a Cocker Spaniel to sit. But there is just something magical about dogs. I've always been fascinated by them and their relatives.

Growing up in a suburb of Minneapolis I was fortunate enough to be exposed to the great work done to save the magnificent wolf. Meeting an actual wolf for the first was a truly spiritual moment for me. Just being in their presence is still nothing short of awe inspiring.

The work of dedicated environmentalist and naturalists was the inspiration that fueled my already developing love of animals – much to the chagrin of my mother. I vividly remember the look on my mom's face when I'd bring home a stray kitten or puppy. My mother was not an animal person to say the least and my ever increasing pleas for a (gasp) puppy were always rebuffed.

My younger brother was born severely handicapped with multiple disabilities. He is still unable to walk and his motor and speech are very limited. Because he required so much care my parents did not want to take on the added responsibility of a dog.

Since I was unable to have a dog first hand I used to read endlessly about them. Everything I could get my hands on about dogs, wolves or other canines was read cover to cover and back again. The more I read about them the more I fell in love with them. How could anyone not want to share their lives with these amazing creatures?

At age thirteen my dad was transferred to his company's Los Angeles office and my family moved to Orange County, California. My dad must have felt really sorry for me leaving all my friends so one day he told my mom, "Shirl' go and get her a dog." I'll never forget the look on my mom's face; it was a combination of horror and disbelief.

For reasons I still don't understand, she did take me out that day to a pet store. After reading countless books on every breed, I wanted a larger dog, perhaps a shepherd mix of some sort. But of course as I would learn over and over again in my life, to quote Mick Jagger, "You don't always get what you want –you get what you need." Apparently what I needed was a little black cockapoo.

Joy of joys, I finally had a dog. Me, with my very own dog! I couldn't have been happier. After much discussion I named the little black fluff ball Pepper. Not very original but I was only thirteen. Finally, I got some first hand experience training, taking care of and loving a dog. That little black ball of fur changed my life. She was the best friend I've ever had.

Me at 13 years old and my Pepper at 8 weeks

We were inseparable to say the least. At ten pounds she was the perfect size to take everywhere. (She really was just what I needed). She went to parties, on dates and was even was in a high school play. I accessorized her accordingly; bandanas, sweaters, collars - she had it all.

When it came time for college I picked one I could attend while living off campus so I could keep her with me. (By that time I also had a cat which is another story). I even had planned for her to be the bouquet at my wedding. How cute would she have been surrounded in floers as I held her walking down the aisle. But the church had some silly rule about no dogs.

Needless to say she was a special little dog that I absolutely adored. On July 3rd, 1989 when she was ten years old, she ran out into the street and was hit by a car and killed. Broken hearted I tried to understand why. I re-evaluated the training that was supposed to have prevented just such a tragedy. This is what sent me on a mission to find better, easier, more reliable ways to teach dogs. A mission I will always continue.

Now, as a mother of two human children I have also learned just how crazy busy a person's life can be. I understand how easily a dog's needs can be pushed to the back burner, but I also know all too well how worthwhile and enriching having a dog can be. My work now is taking my knowledge of dogs and making it easily accessible for crazy busy people too. No one should miss out on the magic that is a dog.

At first, my goal was to spread the gospel of positive reinforcement. It's been almost a century since B.F. Skinner proved positive reinforcement was much more effective at changing behaviors than punishment. Yet incredibly choke chains are still a mainstay of many dog training classes. There is still much work to be done. But, after fifteen years of professional training my goal has mushroomed into not just training dogs, but treasuring them. Not just saving their lives but improving the quality of that life.

What dogs give us far outweighs anything we could ever do for them. Enlighten means to teach, to illuminate, to awaken. A long time ago a little black dog brought light to my life, now it's my turn to awaken that light for you and your dog.
Enlighten Yourself & Then Your Dog!

Chapter 2
First Step to Enlightenment Nourish Your Dog

You are what you eat. Remember learning that in the third grade? Apparently it is truer than we ever imagined. Since losing my dad to cancer almost ten years ago, I've studied the correlation between diet and disease (I plan to be around as long as I can with my children). The connection between what we eat and how healthy we are is proven time and time again. Foods can not only fight disease but make us smarter.

Guess what? This is not only true for humans but for all animals. Nature gives us everything we need to be healthy and it doesn't come in a flashy plastic wrapper. Go to any pet store and you'll see literally aisles of dog foods in nicely packaged cans or bags. It's a billion dollar business. Before WWII most dogs ate table scraps. My dad used to laugh at my expensive pet food purchases. "My dog never ate any of that fancy stuff, and he lived to be twenty." As much as I hate to admit it, my dad was right.

What happened after the war was a lot of social and economic changes and a lot of marketing. The bigger pet food companies spend billions on advertising every year. We have been brainwashed to think proper nutrition can only come from a bag.

The truth about the pet food industry is that it is big business. Ingredients used in most commercial dog food are not fit for human consumption. The food is extruded at such high temperatures most of the nutrition is cooked out of it. Then preservatives are injected into it so it can be shipped all over and sit on shelves for extended periods of time. Besides the nutritional aspect is the ethical one. Some pet food makers actually do animal testing on dogs kept in laboratories. Iams is the main offender, but none of the larger companies have pledged not to participate in the cruel experiments.

What should you feed your dog? If you like the convenience of commercial dog food, look for one that is baked, uses only human quality ingredients and does not engage in animal testing. I also recommend staying away from foods that have wheat or other fillers. A lot of dogs are allergic to the gluten in wheat as well as to other grains. If you notice your dog doing a considerable amount of itching or licking try switching foods.

I feed my own animals *Healthy Pet Net's Life's Abundance*. It is a fantastic dry food that is baked at low temps and delivered fresh to your door - usually within just a few weeks of being made. It is made with fresh, human grade ingredients in a facility that is a USDA certified APHIS (Animal Plant Health Inspection Service) plant. APHIS certification allows the sale of the finished product to the International market, including Europe which has extremely high standards. It also uses only ingredients from the U.S. Check it out at www.fivestarpetfood.com.

Home cooking for your dog is another alternative. You can cook a week's worth of food at one time and freeze it in convenient daily portions. The raw food diet is another option. The B.A.R.F., bones and raw food diet, is closest to what a dog would eat naturally.

The less food is cooked, the more nutrients it retains. This is true for humans too. I personally feed my three dogs and cat a combination of all three; raw food, home cooked and a super premium dry. So far I have heard no complaints.

Bone appetite!

For more information please visit these informative websites:
my-zen-dog.com
fivestarpetfood.com

Chapter 3
Enlighten Yourself & Then Your Dog

Is your dog driving you crazy? Whether he's peeing on your carpet, jumping in your face or thinking the word "come" means run as fast as you can in the other direction; do not lose hope. Your dog is not necessarily an ADD sufferer or mentally unstable. He's just being a dog.

Dogs naturally pee and poop, they naturally jump when excited and generally love a good game of catch me if you can. Actually they love a good game of anything and depending on your dog, can be very skilled at training you to play along. So how do you turn the tables and teach them to follow *your* rules. It is actually quite easy if you keep a few things in mind as you teach and live with them.

First of all, remember that any behavior that is followed by something positive will be repeated. The more you reward the behavior the more frequently your dog will do it. What does your dog find rewarding? This will vary slightly from dog to dog, but generally dogs find food, toys, attention, and so on rewarding.

So the next time your dog jumps on you and you pet him, you are telling him, "thank you for jumping this is a good way to get my attention." Of course your dog does not know jumping on you is o.k. when you are wearing jeans but not o.k. when you are wearing dress pants. If you don't want him to jump, don't reward him for it. Pushing him away and yelling when he jumps can also be a reward. He got your attention didn't he? If your dog is doing something you don't like, jumping for instance, don't reward it. Second, replace the bad habit with a good one. Just saying "no" all the time doesn't really teach him what he should do. So teach him. If you don't want your dog to jump to greet you, what do you want him to do?

Usually we teach the behavior "sit". He can't be jumping if he is sitting; this is a mutually exclusive behavior. He cannot be doing one when he is doing the other. The more he learns sit works and jump doesn't the more he will sit for your attention even when you don't ask him. I think this is the dog's way of saying "please" and "thank you".

To teach your dog to sit all you need are some tasty treats and some patience. The treats should be about pea size and something he really likes. You can even use your dog's regular food as treat, as long as he will work for it. Motivation is the key to successful learning. If your dog does not like the treat much, he won't play along. Food is like money to your dog. A piece of dry kibble is probably worth $5; a piece of jerky may be worth $50, a little piece of cheese or leftover turkey maybe worth $1000 or more. Think of you would not do for $5, you would at least think about for $1,000,000.

Take a treat and put it on your dog's nose. Let him sniff the tasty morsel as you move it slowly between his eyes, backwards towards his tail. As he follows the treat over his head his hindquarters are going to touch the ground. If he remains standing or moves backwards just be patient and try again. Remember this is trial and error learning, meaning your dog has no idea what you want him to do so it may take a few repetitions. Resist the temptation to push on his back end. This may be confusing and actually inhibit learning. Also, we want him to use his brain to figure out what we want so he learns how to play the training game.

As your dog's tail (or stump depending on your dog's breed) touches the ground say, "Good sit" and give him the treat. Repeat this several times until you are able to just use the hand motion without the treat to get this behavior. Now your dog knows sit. This is a fundamental command that will help you build on further training. Have your dog sit for everything he wants; food, toys, attention. This will help you to train your dog throughout the day without really thinking about it. This is also a great leadership exercise to let your dog know you are the boss and to reward him for listening to you.

Remember training is a game. Reward your dog often and have fun!

Dogs are not democratic and it is against their nature to share. Dogs look for a definite hierarchy and pecking order. Leaders lead and followers follow. If you do not prove yourself to be a leader, your dog will assume the role even if he may not want to.

All humans in a dog's pack (family) must establish themselves as leaders from the start. As soon as you bring a new dog into your home (pack) you must establish yourself as leader. Many common problems can be prevented if human leadership is established from the beginning. But setting yourself up as leader does not and should not involve any physical or aggressive techniques. Leadership can be proven through very effective yet passive means.

Leadership

Leadership is the basis of all training. Just like children, dogs need to know who is in charge. A leader must be confident, dependable, firm and kind.

Leadership is accomplished through the following passive methods:

Early and consistent training. Give your puppy the same rules that he will have when he is fully grown. It is tempting to let a small puppy jump up for attention but it is unfair to get mad at him for doing the same behavior when he is bigger. It is easier to prevent bad habits than it is to stop them. Teach the rules from day one.

Restraint/handling exercises. Actively teach your dog to love to be handled. Touch his ears, give him a treat. Touch his paws, give him a treat. Touch his tail, give him a treat. He will learn to love to be touched all over. This is important throughout his life ensuring that all medical examination will be stress free and never lead to defensive (aggressive) behaviors. He will not need sedation should your dog require more invasive medical treatment as he ages. If your dog struggles when you hold him do not release him until he is settled. If he struggles and you put him down he learns that struggling works. Teach him settling works.

Learn to earn training. Nothing is free. Your dog must work (perform behaviors) for all life rewards. Every time you ask your dog to "sit" and he complies, he is submitting to you. Even a small child (with your help) can teach a dog basic commands.

Humans eat first. In a pack it is the dominant members that eat first. The subordinates must wait their turn according to their rank. Of course in the

human family the dog is always last and should be the last to eat.

Teach your dog to "move" when he is blocking your path. Don't go around the dog, make him move for you by gently shuffling your feet under him until he moves. (This also comes in handy if you have an armful of groceries or a baby and cannot see the dog. He learns to look out for you.) Motivational training not punishment based training clearly teaches your dog his place in his pack family and how to behave there.

Communication – dog talk
When you live with a dog it is like living with someone who speaks a different language and has different (sometimes very different) customs. We cannot teach your dog to speak your human language, so we must learn his. This does not mean you have to get down on all fours and woof at him.

But you can look at situations from his point of view. Are you really conveying the message you want or is your dog taking it another way? For instance when the puppy piddles on the rug and the owner rushes over, picks him up and coos, "No, no, no. Mommy doesn't like it when you do that." What is the owner *really* telling the puppy?

Another mistake can be pushing your dog away when he jumps up on you. The dog can see this as a

game and simply return for more.
If your dog is doing something that bugs you, whether it's jumping, house soiling or chewing the first step in correcting it is to objectively step back and ask yourself, "How is this behavior being rewarded?" "Am I or someone else, rewarding this?" Make sure you are telling your dog what you want him to know.

Dogs can and do read our emotions. Remember your dog is a predator. Even inside little fluffy couch-dweller beats the heart of a predator. Your dog has extremely keen senses. He can hear your heartbeat, smell you sweat and of course he is very adept at reading your body language. If you are tense it is a sure bet your dog knows this and may also tense up. It is call the interpretive factor. (Remember this point when discussing aggression prevention.)

How to Reward

The reward must immediately follow the desired behavior. If you wait more than two seconds (one second with puppies and Border Collies) you are probably rewarding something else. If you ask your dog to "sit" and three seconds after they sit they raise their paw – then you reward them. What they learn is that "sit" means put your bottom on the ground and raise a paw. Watch your timing.

A reward is anything your dog wants – meals, treats, toys, and attention. One of the many

wonderful benefits of reward training is that you can actually see your dog think.

How to Reprimand

Get out of the habit of saying "no". We say it all the time and they learn to tune it out (so do children). If your dog acts inappropriately say a sharp, "ah ah" in a firm reprimand tone. This usually gets their attention and you can then give them an instructive reprimand such as "off" or "outside". Tell them what to do. Another problem with the use of the word "no" is that it doesn't tell the dog what is the correct thing to do. Save your "no's" and if you must use them say it like you mean in a room shaking, "NO!"

Environmental corrections or remote corrections can also be beneficial. This is a spray of water from a small squirt bottle or the startling effect of a well-thrown shaker can. (A shaker can is an empty aluminum can rinsed out with three-six pennies in it and duct tape over the hole so the pennies don't fall out when it is thrown.) You will want to throw the shaker can at your dog, not to hit him but to land next to him. It is the sound and the motion that will startle your dog and build an aversion to the inappropriate behavior he is exhibiting when you throw the can.

The trick when using these props is to be discreet. Don't let the dog see you with the bottle or the can. If he knows you have it he will learn not to do the behavior only when you have the can.

For instance if your dog jumps up on visitors take the can to the door with you holding it behind your back. As the dog *begins* to jump toss the can and walk away. You want your dog to think it was the wall or the couch that threw it. So even when you are not around he will not jump. Remember punishment alone only teaches the dog to avoid the punishment not the behavior.

In addition to using these reprimands you must follow up by teaching your dog the correct way to behave in that situation. In this scenario work with your dog so that he sits before he is greeted. He cannot jump if he is sitting. Make an aversion to the wrong behavior through use of the remote correction but also teach the correct behavior.

Tones of Voice
How you say something, especially when beginning training, is just as important as what you say.

The three tones of voice:
Command
Praise
Reprimand

Your dog will be less confused and learn much faster if your body language and tone of voice coincide with the command you consistently use.

Basic Training
Life Learning
Actively work on commands with your dog at least thirty minutes a day. The more you work with your dog the faster he will progress. There are no short

cuts to this step. However, do not work with your dog for more than five to ten minutes at a time.

Break your training into three to four short sessions instead of one long session. Integrate training into your life. Your dog must work for all life rewards. He must do a sit, down, come, or any combination of commands for everything he finds rewarding in life. Things such as food, attention, toys are all items your dog values. Make him earn them. This makes the commands much more meaningful for your dog and helps you to get in your thirty minutes of training a day. It also makes it just as much of a habit for you to ask your dog to behave properly and politely as it is for him to behave that way.

Initially use food treats every time your dog correctly responds to a new command. Once your dog consistently responds correctly to the new command, then begin to give treats every second or third time and than taper off even more the better he gets. Give "jackpot" rewards occasionally for best responses. This will keep your dog excited about training. Always verbally praise a correct response as well as good behavior.

Save petting as a "jackpot" or "bonus" reward at the end of a training session. This is especially important when first beginning training or teaching a new behavior. Touching can be distracting and confusing for your dog. It can also get him too excited and therefore distract him from the learning at hand.

Don't let your dog train you.
Whether he is an eight week old purebred puppy or an eight year old rescue dog, establish household rules the first day that you adopt your dog. Give your puppy the same rules he will have as an adult. It is not fair to let your cute little six pound pup jump up to greet you and then yell at him when he does the same thing when he is sixty pounds. *It is much easier to prevent a bad habit than it is to break one.*

Always replace a bad habit with a good one.
If your dog is doing something that bugs you, the second question (the first again is "what is the reward?") to ask yourself is, "What do I *want* my dog to do in this situation?" If your dog is jumping up to greet you; teach him to sit for greetings. If your dog has taken a liking to peeing on your living room carpet, teach him to pee outside on the grass.

Think positively – *teach what you want.*
Keep your cool with your dog. You will greatly set back your training and your relationship with your

dog if you get angry and resort to physical punishments. Dogs respond best to clear, reliable, consistent and kind leadership.

Under absolutely no circumstances should you hit

or inflict pain on your dog in any way.

Dogs do not hit each other with newspapers, flyswatters or anything else. They do not understand this and you can actually be creating a lot of problems. If you get angry at your dog for whatever reason it is best to leave the room until you feel better and can deal with finding a solution rationally.

Teach your dog to behave quietly and politely indoors. Use a tether if needed and always give your dog a good chewy to passively teach him to lie down and chew his toy nicely while inside. Be patient. Learning happens through many repetitions and in many different situations.

Dogs are good discriminators but poor generalizes. Which means you need to work with your dog in many situations and in many locations for your dog to generalize the learning. Just because your dog knows "sit" in the living room doesn't necessarily mean he knows it in the kitchen. Or, if you are the only one that works with your dog, he may not respond as well (if at all) to your spouse. Learning is an ongoing process that does take time.

Keep your dog healthy and well exercised. Many health problems have behavior-related symptoms.

Also, keep in mind that there may be underlying physiological reasons for behavior problems. For instance some dogs experience housebreaking set backs after undergoing anesthetic or having urinary tract infections. Internal parasites can also be the cause of uncontrollable house soiling. Diabetes can make a usually well-behaved dog so ravenous he will steal food and his increased thirst will cause him to have accidents in the house. Work with your veterinarian and behaviorist as a team.

Teaching Commands
Say the command one time. The command is "sit" not "sit, sit, sit". Be careful not to repeat yourself. Sometimes we do it without even realizing it, but you dog certainly does. Watch what you say, when you say it and how you say it.

Always praise the correct response whether or not you are using a food reward. Say "good" as your dog does the behavior, not as you are giving him the food. Timing is crucial. Praise your dog while he is performing the desired behavior.

Teach and then test. Just because he does it once, doesn't mean that he knows it. Practice sequences in short sessions in many different situations. Dogs are poor at generalizing so you need to practice the commands in many different locations and in many different positions. Safety is always first. Never work with your dog off-leash in an unconfined area. Even the best trained dogs make mistakes.

Always end your training sessions on positive responses. Keep the training fun. Working with your dog should be fun. You didn't get a dog because you needed more work in your life. You got him to bring you more joy. If it ceases to be fun enlist the help of a professional trainer. Ask your friends or veterinarian for a recommendation. The Association of Pet Dog Trainers website, www.apdt.com, is a good resource to find a qualified trainer in your area.

Why Reward-Based Training
It works. By rewarding your dog for correct responses you increase the likelihood that that behavior will re-occur and re-occur more frequently. Punishment, on the other hand, does not teach correct behavior. It only teaches the organism how to avoid the punishment. A reward is anything your dog likes – food, toys, balls, attention, etc. Use a variety of rewards to keep your dog interested and motivated. Work away from the food rewards by increasing the use of other rewards. Only if *you* get stuck using the food will your dog get stuck needing it.

Through the use of positive reinforcement the end result is a dog that responds consistently to your commands, is well adjusted and is able to meet their full potential. Remember your dog is not a machine. He is a living, thinking entity that routinely makes behavior choices - just like you. By rewarding the behaviors you want, the dog will choose them more often. No coercion, force or punishment is necessary. If you make it worth the dog's while to behave a certain way – he will.

Think of it not as "training" your dog—but rather "teaching" your dog. You are teaching your dog the correct way to behave as he lives in your family. But this teaching does not have to be boring and tedious—it should be fun. Keep your sessions short and as with everything, always keep your sense of humor.

Chapter 4
Inside Dog vs. Outside Dog

Once you adopt a dog or puppy, you and your family become his pack. A dog requires consistent and stable contact with his pack. If a dog is isolated from his pack, you, he may become anxious. This anxiety can display itself in behaviors such as destructive chewing, digging or barking and whining. This anxiety can be caused by the owner's absence as with separation anxiety or simply by boredom and lack of stimulation. If the dog is relegated to the outdoors and has minimal human contact his anxiety may increase to escape behaviors.

An outside dog is virtually impossible to house train. The more time he spends outside the more he will eliminate wherever and whenever he feels the urge. This, of course, lessens your opportunity to reward. It is a vicious cycle that happens. If the dog is not properly taught how to behave inside, it is easiest for the owner just to put him outside. When he allowed back in again he becomes very excited at the chance to be with you again and all the new sights and smells inside. Therefore in his glee he will run around wildly jumping on people and furniture. This scene will undoubtedly find him outside again.

Believe it or not it is much easier to train a dog to behave inside than to behave outside. You can break the outside dog cycle simply by redirecting all that exuberance into a positive behavior like chewing a bone. Have a nice meaty sterilized bone or a Kong ball stuffed with treats and offer it to your dog as you bring him inside. He will take the bone or Kong lie down and chew to his heart's content.

If a dog has been outside for a long time he may be too excited to take the treats. Play ball or take him for a long walk to tire him out before bringing him inside. Then give him something extra special to chew on when he is inside.

Bringing your dog inside will allow him to be truly part of the family and the companion dog he was meant to be.

Chapter 5
House training

This is a step-by-step guide to help you understand and be successful throughout the process of house training your dog. The steps are the same regardless of your dog's age, breed, sex or temperament.

House training is the most important behavior your dog needs to learn to live with you. If the dog is not successfully housebroken he will be relegated to living his life outdoors. If your dog is outside he is not a true companion for you. Dogs, as pack animals need our companionship as much as we need theirs. Isolation from his pack (you) can lead to stress which will manifest itself in other behavior problems such as digging, chewing (on themselves as well) and vocalization (barking, howling, whining). House training your dog correctly is one of the nicest things you can do for your dog and yourself.

The keys to house training are consistency and timing. If you are consistent and have good timing, you can teach your dog to be completely housebroken in seven days. I've been able to train some dogs in five days.

To housebreak your dog in one week you must focus completely on housebreaking. Follow the steps to the letter and do not go faster than what your dog is capable of doing. If your dog has an accident - learn from it.

Either you went too quickly or need to follow the steps closer, whatever the reason he simply did not learn the correct place to eliminate. Don't read too much into the accident other than your dog has not yet learned the lesson.

Remember dogs are not vindictive or spiteful. They do not, at least there is no scientific proof, have emotions like anger. Therefore they do not pee and poop on our carpet because they are mad at us. Sometimes it may seem as though your dog's pooping on the floor is his way of saying, "take that", but it is simply not the case.

There are six basic steps to house training. These are the same steps used by the top trainers and behaviorists not only to train their clients' dogs but also to train their own dogs. Read the steps a couple of times until you feel comfortable and confident with them - then begin.

Chapter 6
The 6 Steps to Successfully House training Your Dog

1.   Start With A Healthy Dog
step number one in teaching your dog anything is to make sure he is healthy. A dog of any age can learn as long as they are in good health. Internal parasites and urinary tract infections can make it difficult if not impossible for your dog to control his bowel and bladder. Anesthesia may also affect your dog's ability to control elimination as with some medication. It is not uncommon for a dog, especially a puppy, to regress in house training after surgery.

2.   Regulate Input & Output
Put bluntly, if you know when something goes into your dog you can anticipate when it will come out of your dog. So, regulate your dog's food and water. Give your dog fifteen to twenty minutes to eat and pick-up whatever food is left. Also monitor your dog's water intake. Watch your dog's water intake

carefully and use common sense. In warm weather or if your dog is active he will need to drink more often. If your dog is outside all day he will need access to water at all times. But if your dog is inside offer him water every hour or so depending on the weather and your dog's activity level.

You need to monitor when your dog eats or drinks anything so you can get him to the right place at the right time to eliminate and reward him for it. That is the entire goal of house training.

Make a house training chart. Write down the time and what your dog consumed. Then write down the time you took him out and if he defecated or urinated. If you have two or more dogs that you are training, make each one their own chart. Writing it down helps you to see any patterns that have developed and it helps keep you consistent. If your dog has an accident be sure to write it down in red ink.

3.   Confine & Supervise

Confinement and supervision are extremely important to the success of housebreaking your dog. I cannot stress enough the importance of this step at this stage in your dog's training. Never allow your dog, especially a puppy, to roam in your house unsupervised for even two seconds. Two seconds is plenty of time for him to sneak behind the sofa and poop. It is also plenty of time to chew a shoe or do some other equally typical and equally annoying puppy thing. When you are unable to watch your dog 100% you must confine him.

Confinement can be as simple as tethering your dog on his leash to the couch with a nice chewy. Or you can even tether your dog to yourself; this also helps with the bonding process. Of course, tethering should only be done while you are there to supervise your dog. Never ever leave a dog tethered unattended as he may strangle himself.

When you are gone you can confine your dog in a small room such as a bathroom or laundry room. Leave him preferably somewhere with floors that are easy to clean in case there is an accident. I recommend using a baby gate to enclose the dog as opposed to shutting the door, which can create a barrier frustration. Crate training your dog is also beneficial. I recommend the plastic kennel as opposed to the wire cage variety. Dogs are naturally den animals and feel more secure when they have the three sides covered.

Whatever your preference for confinement practice it while you are home. Put your dog in his "room" with several toys. I suggest a couple of Kong balls stuffed with a little kibble and peanut butter to keep him busy. Never let your dog out of his enclosure while he is barking or whining. Remember rule number one – don't reward behaviors you don't want repeated.

If you are going to be gone for more than four to five hours, (depending on the age of your dog and how long they can hold their bladder and bowel) have a dog walker or a neighbor take your dog out to potty. The more you can prevent accidents from happening, the faster your dog will be conditioned to go in his pee zone.

Paper training is not necessary. I don't recommend it unless your dog will be using newspaper as his permanent pee zone. It's easier to teach your dog right away to go on the surface he will be using the rest of his life. Who has time for another step? Skip the paper training unless you have some real reason to do it.

You also do not need "puppy pads" which serve the same purpose as newspaper only more absorbent and a lot more expensive. Most puppies use these pads as chew toys and just create another mess for you to clean up.

4.   Reward! Reward! Reward!
Get to know your dog's biological idiosyncrasies. Does your dog have to urinate fifteen minutes after drinking water or is it thirty minutes? Does your dog have to defecate fifteen minutes after eating or

is it more like forty-five minutes? Some dogs are "double dumpers", they pee and poop and fifteen minutes later they have to poop again. One of my dogs is a "delayed pooper". He pees and exactly fifteen minutes later he has to poop. Know your dog. If you are regulating his food and water it should be easy to see his elimination patterns. When you think your dog has to go, take him to the spot where you want him to go every time. If you consistently take him to this spot and reward him for going there, this becomes his pee zone. Teach your dog to eliminate on command by saying "get busy" or "tinkle tinkle", or whatever word or phrase you want to use, as your dog is doing that behavior. If you are consistent with the word your dog will associate that command with that action. It is just like teaching sit or down. I do not, however, recommend using commands such as "go potty" or "hurry up". These are phrases you may tell a child or someone else and the dog may obediently eliminate on your living room rug. Choose your command words carefully.

The most important thing to remember in rewarding your dog is timing. The reward has to come immediately following the desired behavior. If you hesitate you may be rewarding something else. The biggest mistake made in house training, other than not confining, is in the timing. Don't stand at the door and then give the dog a treat when he comes in – that is rewarding him for coming. Go out with the

Don't play with him; just stand there very low key. He is there to do a job, play with him as part of the reward for a job well done. As your dog finishes his business, plop a couple of extra yummy food treats in his mouth. Give him the treat just as he finishes his job. Praise is wonderful but food gets the message across a lot faster.

5.   Reprimand in The Act *ONLY*

Never, I don't care how mad you get, hit your dog. If you need to, put your dog outside until you cool down. Hitting only teaches your dog things you don't want him to learn, like aggression. Trust me; don't hit your dog.

Delayed punishment does not work. Let me repeat that – delayed punishment does *not* work. Reprimands must occur during the act. This is true not only for housebreaking but also for all behaviors. Delayed punishment, even a few seconds after the behavior, is confusing and will cause problems. Use sounds and motion to correct your dog. Clap your hands, stomp your feet and in a low reprimand tone tell your dog, "outside" and immediately escort your dog out to his pee zone.

If you have a small dog, resist the temptation to just pick them up and take them to the pee zone. They need to learn to go there on their own and in some instances picking the dog up may be a reward.

Hopefully when you get your dog to the pee zone he has a little left and finishes his job there so you can amply reward him.

If your dog has an accident - learn from it. It means you need to watch your dog closer. Go back and review the previous steps, especially step number two (no pun intended).

6. Odor Neutralize

If your dog has had an accident you must use a good odor neutralizer to clean it up. Regular carpet cleaners cover up the odor so our simple noses can't smell it, but your dog can. The lingering scent of urine or feces many remind him (or any visiting dogs for that matter) to use that spot again. I recommend using commercial products such as Nature's Miracle or Outright. White vinegar mixed 50/50 with water works well too and clears up your sinuses at the same time.

Consistency

Consistency is key to successfully and quickly house training your dog. Set up a strict schedule and follow it rigorously. Remember that as your dog gets better you can loosen up little by little. But if he has an accident just go backwards a little, confine him more and also really focus on those rewards. Make it worth his while to go in the pee zone and nowhere else.

The more consistent you are with these six steps the faster your dog will learn where and when to pee and poop.

Review these steps when you take your dog to other homes and public places. Remember dogs are poor at generalizing. So, just because he knows not to eliminate in your home does not necessarily mean he knows not to eliminate at Grandma's. Just watch him close and reward him for going outside at other houses and you'll be fine.

The Next Step

After your dog is consistently eliminating in his pee zone without accidents, then it is time to go to the next step. Teaching your dog to tell you he has to go out is relatively easy as long as you are consistent. How you want your dog to *tell* you he has to go is up to you. For obvious reasons I don't recommend encouraging your dog to scratch at the door. My own dogs bark at the door once when they have to go out. Or you could teach your dog to ring a bell. The method is entirely up to you.

To teach your dog to bark at the door to get your attention you simply have him sit and speak every time you let him out. Going out to relieve himself actually is a reward in itself, so make him work for it. If you are consistent with whatever method you decide upon, your dog will catch on to it. But don't rely on the dog to *tell* you he has to go out until later on in his training.

If your dog has an accident, especially if you are trying to go to the next step, just watch him closer. You went a little ahead of what he was ready to do that's all. Your dog is not being spiteful or vengeful if he has an accident; he just has not learned yet.

Teach "Speak" or *"Let me out I gotta pee"*
To teach your dog to "speak" set-up the stimulus that makes him bark. For instance, if your dog barks when someone rings the doorbell use that as the stimulus. Go to the door and ring the bell. As soon as your dog barks you say, "good speak," and give him a treat. Repeat this a couple of times than you say "speak" – ring the bell – the dog barks – you say "good speak" – give him a treat. The dog is learning that speak means bark and he's rewarded for that behavior. After a couple of repetitions you can drop the stimulus (the doorbell) and simply say "speak" and the dog will bark.

Remember that dogs are visually learners. Your body language is easier for them to learn than the spoken word. So when you teach your dog something new always incorporate a hand sign from the start. They actually learn the hand sign before they learn the verbal cue. For speak I just open and close my hand quickly as a hand sign.
If you teach your dog to speak you must teach them the command "quiet". Quiet means stop barking so

have your dog speak and then say "quiet" while putting a treat on his nose. Your dog cannot bark and sniff the treat at the same time – try it it's impossible. After he has been quiet for two seconds give him the treat and say, "good quiet". Give your dog another treat, praise again.

After you teach your dog to speak it is very important you don't reward your dog for speaking unless you ask him. Otherwise your dog will learn barking is a great way to get your attention, whether you like it or not.

Submissive & Excited Urination

Submissive urination is an instinctive behavior dogs exhibit to show extreme submission. Usually a dog will roll over on his back showing his belly first which in itself is an overtly submissive act. The dog will then begin to drip a little urine as if to say, "I'm such a worm. I'm as low as I can possibly get." If your dog submissively urinates whatever you do, do not reprimand him for this.

If you reprimand him at all you are likely to end up with more peeing as the dog tries to be even more submissive. It is a vicious cycle that happens so don't even start it. Usually if you just turn away from the dog he will stop because you are no longer a threat. If he continues, just take him outside in a very calm, neutral manner.

Excited urination happens when the dog become so stimulated it cannot hold its bladder. This usually happens during greetings. If this is the case keep your greetings very low key. Even so much as to ignore the dog completely for the first ten or fifteen minutes after arriving home. After the fifteen minutes have the dog sit nicely and then greet him in a very calm, neutral manner. You may want to do this outside for the first couple times or so, just in case. If your dog exhibits exited urination upon greeting guests, have your guests greet the dog in the same before mentioned manner.

Sometimes puppies will grow out of this behavior. But to be on the safe side, practice low-key greetings. What starts out as a physiological response can become a learned habit. It's always easier to prevent a bad habit than it is to correct one.

Frequently Asked Questions
"My dog is three years old and has never been housebroken. Is there still hope?"
Absolutely. These steps are the same for dogs of all ages. If your dog is healthy he can learn. The only difference age makes is that it takes longer. A four month-old puppy may take a few days to learn a new behavior, whereas a four-year-old dog may take a few months. But each dog is an individual and learns at his or her own pace.

Also, the older dog may have bad habits you need to break as you teach new good ones.

"My dog pees outside, then after I bring him in, he pees again."
Know that about your dog. Anticipate his routine and set him up to succeed. Bring him inside and watch him 100% or confine him. After a couple of minutes inside, take him back outside to finish – and reward him.

"My two year old male dog likes to mark on the furniture. Help!"
Marking is a little different that simple housebreaking. Your dog is not just eliminating but leaving a visual and scent mark. First and foremost you must have your dog neutered. Without neutering him you are fighting an uphill battle. The behavior can be controlled without the surgery but it is difficult and not a topic for a novice. I suggest working with a Behaviorist if you have an intact male and want to keep him that way.
If your dog has been neutered, give him a "pee post" and reward him for marking there. Any vertical object will do as a pee post. A stick, pipe or a particular tree all will work. You can entice your dog to mark there by taping a couple of Q-tips you previously dipped in your neighbor's dog's urine to the post. The steps of house training are the same for marking, but incorporate a pee post or two in your yard to give your dog a visual marker for him to,

well, mark.

Spaying and neutering your dog is one the best things you can do for your dog. It will prevent reproductive cancers, certain behavior problems and ease the tragedy of unwanted puppies.

Chapter 7
Separation Anxiety

Being pack animals, and therefore highly social, dogs are prone to develop separation anxiety. Separation anxiety is when an individual becomes stressed in the absence of another individual or group. This anxiety can manifest itself as destructive chewing, vocalizations such as howling and barking, elimination accidents and escape behaviors.

The steps to alleviate separation anxiety are the same to prevent it. Since it is always easier to prevent something than to cure it, I encourage you to practice the following steps to teach your dog to be alone.

Low-key arrivals and departures. Ignore your dog for the first fifteen to twenty minutes when leaving or arriving home.
Practice leaving. When you are staying home make a point of putting your dog in the area where he is

confined in your absence with plenty of toys for
five to ten minutes several times a day.
Redirect attention & reward absence. When you
leave your dog alone literally litter his area with
toys. Make it doggie Disneyland so he will have
many correct items to chew on if he becomes anxious.
Also save some particularly good ones that he
only gets when he is alone. For instance a nice
Kong ball stuffed with treats and maybe even a little
peanut butter. This will actually reward him for being
alone.

Getting another dog does not prevent or
alleviate separation anxiety. Unless you are
following the above steps you will probably have
two dogs with separation anxiety.

Chapter 8
Chewing

Teach your dog the correct items to chew.
Plan to spend $50 to $200 on chew toys. It is
a lot less expensive than a new couch or carpet or
even a couple of pairs of shoes. Recommended
chew toys include the Kong ball, Nylabone and
natural sterilized bone just to name a few.

Any toy that has a hole, put food into it to passively
teach your dog to like it. Kong balls are great for this.
Squeak toys are not good chew toys. They are great
for training sessions but please do not leave your
dog alone with them to chew. Many dogs will chew
the squeaker out and eat it and may also ingest
particles of plastic.

Other items not recommended are; rawhides that get
soggy when chewed and may cause an obstruction
and cow hooves that may also cause an obstruction.
Animal products such as cow hooves, pigs' ears and
snouts may also carry bacteria such as salmonella.

Kongs come in a size for all dogs.

This is definitely a concern especially if there are children in the house.

Actively teach your dog to chew his toys. Buying a bunch of toys does not ensure your dog will want to chew them. Offer your dog one of his toys; praise him profusely when he even touches it. Offer your dog one of your toys, like a shoe or remote control. If he touches your toy, reprimand him with a sharp, "ah ah" or "off".

Keep a bin full of your dog's toys where he has access to them at all times. Encourage him to go to his bin, if he touches a toy- praise him. Offer him a toy from his bin and praise him when he takes it. You can even pair his toy with a food treat for further impact. Rotate his toys. Put a favorite toy in the closet for a couple of days and when you offer it to your dog again it will be like a brand new toy. Supervise or confine your dog at all times until you have established a good chew toy habit. Do not allow a young puppy or new dog into unsupervised areas of the house until he has proven himself worthy. Keep your dog in the bedroom with you at night in a crate, exercise pen or on a tie down.

When you are home to supervise you can tether the dog to your chair or to yourself so he cannot sneak off and chew. In your absence confine your dog to a small bathroom laundry room or crate and literally litter the area with Kongs stuffed with food and other appropriate toys.

If you catch your dog chewing on something he shouldn't, reprimand him with a sharp, "ah ah" or "off". Wait about 5 seconds (so you are not inadvertently rewarding him for chewing incorrectly) and then usher him over to his toy bin and offer him a toy. When he takes the toy praise him. Remember to always replace a bad habit with a good one.

Teach your dog what he *can* chew.
Taste Aversion. "Bitter Apple" and other taste aversions can be used to put on articles your dog has already taken a liking to chewing. Most sprays are alcohol based so they will evaporate fairly quickly. There are, however, also pastes available at any feed or pet store that are long lasting.

Chapter 9
Walking on Leash

To teach your dog to walk nicely by your side you will need several pieces of equipment. Of course you will need a leash. I recommend a six foot one. The four footers always seem to be a little short especially for the smaller dogs. The retractable leashes will actually teach your dog to pull as they give him so much leash you have very little control. It really doesn't matter if the leash is leather or nylon, just a personal preference.

You will also need a fantastic motivator. Selecting a good motivator is key to your success. Difficulty with leash walking occurs because there are literally millions of distractions just on a walk around the block. Since distractions are technically just competing motivators make sure you have a really good one on your side. Special yummy treats work well as do squeaky toys. Retriever owners remember- to never underestimate the power of a tennis ball to hold your dog's interest.

The last piece of equipment you will need is a collar. A regular buckle collar is fine; you do not need a choke chain. I want the dog to walk nicely with me because he wants to, not because I am choking it out of him. Besides, no matter how much I lift weights there is no way I can out muscle a Rottweiller. Sometimes a Yorkshire terrier can be tricky as well. For most breeds the neck and chest area is the strongest part of the dog, so when we use a choke chain we are trying to control them at their strongest point.

This usually doesn't work. We humans then become conditioned to trying to control them physically, we usually fail. I want you to break that habit. Think of the leash, as a safety device only for security purposes, not control. If your dog is a habitual puller, he has been doing it for years or after you try the following technique still have a problem with pulling; then I suggest using a Gentle Leader.

A Gentle Leader on a dog

A Gentle Leader is a head harness for your dog much like a bridle for a horse. You would never put a choke chain on a horse and expect to be able to control them. Though they may be smaller, some dogs are as strong as a horse.

The Gentle Leader goes around the dog's nose and attaches behind his ears. The leash then attaches to a loop under the dog's chin. This is the weakest area on the dog and he must follow where his nose goes, making pulling physically impossible. If the dog starts to pull you just stop and the dog cannot pull. When your dog is on the Gentle Leader you must be careful not to do any type of leash correction because it may injure their neck. Canine Companions and many other organizations are using Gentle Leader's on all their dogs. It is a five minute miracle in a box.

Now that you have the equipment, the next step in teaching your dog to walk nicely with you is to pick a side. It doesn't matter if your dog is on the left or the right, whichever side is most comfortable for you just be consistent. If your dog is on the left he is always on the left unless of course you teach the command "right" or vise versa. This way your dog will automatically stay on that side and not weave back and forth causing you to trip.

If your dog is on your left side, for example, you want to hold the leash in your right hand. That way the leash comes across your body and you have some leverage should you need it. Place the loop of leash over your right thumb and grasp it with your fist. Never wrap the leash around your wrist. Holding it in your hand gives you more control whereas wrapping it around you wrist may cause an injury, especially if your dog sees a cat and jerks you unexpectedly.

Whenever your dog is on leash always keep the leash nice and loose. It should hang by your dog's shoulder but be careful he does not trip on it. There should never be any pressure from the collar on your dog's neck. The more he feels his collar pull the more he will become used to it so leash corrections will become less and less effective.

If your dog starts to pull and the leash begins to get tight, just stop. Plant your feet so that your dog cannot go forward. If your dog is able to pull just one inch closer to where he wants to go, then pulling works. First rule of training is not to reward a behavior you don't want. Make sure pulling does not work.

At this point you can wait for there to be slack in the leash again, and then continue your walk. If the dog begins to pull, stop again. You can either continue to do this or employ your motivator to help facilitate the process. If your dog is on your left side, hold a treat or toy in your left hand at nose level to your dog. (You little dog owners may have to bend over a bit for this, but it is only temporary.) If your dog jumps to get the motivator just lower it. You are conditioning your dog to walk at your side even when you stop using treats.

With a nice loose leash take a few steps then stop and lure the treat or toy over your dog's head until he sits. Praise and give him a treat. Take a few more steps, stop and lure a treat or toy over your dog's head until he sits. Praise and give him a treat. Repeat many times until your dog sits automatically when you stop. I just think that is polite. As you walk with your dog don't forget to praise him frequently when he is walking nicely. Let him know what a good job he is doing. Use the motivator to keep him by your side and make sure the pulling does not work.

Chapter 10
Understanding Barking

Dogs naturally chew, dig, poop and bark.
These are all extremely normal canine behaviors.
It is only when they live with us that they
must learn what to chew, where to poop and when
to bark. Your dog has many different types of barks.
He will bark to get inside/outside, to get your
attention, in fear or frustration and of course as an
alarm signal.

Dogs *should* bark when someone comes to your
door. It is their job to let you know "hey, there's
somebody out there" and to let the other person
know, "hey there's a dog in here." Studies show
that even the smallest dog is a deterrent to crime.
That alarm bark is probably one big reason our
primitive ancestors encouraged our dogs' primitive
ancestors to start hanging around in the first place.

As wonderful as the alarm bark is, however, your
dog does need to obey your command of "quiet" or
"shush" as well. It is his job as the subordinate in

the pack to let the leader (you) know there is possible danger but he should stop when told to stop.

The first step to control your dog's barking is to make sure it is not being rewarded. If your dog is outside and you let him in when he barks; he learns barking works. If your dog barks at you and you talk to him; he learns barking is a great way to get your attention. Be careful not to comfort your dog while he is barking by petting and talking soothingly to him. This is essentially telling him, "good dog thank your for barking." Picking up little dogs when they bark is a sure fire way to get them to bark again. Watch the way you and others respond to your dog when he barks. *Do not reward behaviors you do not want repeated.*

Second step to control barking is to actually teach your dog to bark on cue. If you teach your dog to "speak" on cue you can then teach him the all important command, "quiet." As discussed in the housebreaking section, to teach your dog to bark on command set up the stimulus that causes that behavior.

The doorbell is usually good for this. Ring the bell; your dog barks; say "good speak" and give him a treat. Repeat this several times until you can fade out the bell and simply say, "speak" to initiate a bark. You can even throw in a hand sign to make it easier for you and your dog to catch on to this. Do not reward "speak" unless you ask for it. Dogs are very adept at training us to pay attention when they bark. Don't fall for it.

Once your dog knows "speak" you must teach him "quiet". The command "quiet" means stop barking. So, to teach this have your dog "speak" and then place a treat on his nose to distract him. Say "quiet" then praise him and give him the treat when he stops barking. Put your index finger to your mouth as a hand sign to help your dog learn this. Repeat this several times until your dog is consistently exhibiting the desired behavior – silence. Teach the correct behavior.

Now that you have effectively taught your dog the "quiet" command, you can enforce it. Use an environmental correction such as a spray bottle full of water or a shaker can as a consequence for continuing to bark. Say the command first; if your dog stops barking praise him. If your dog continues to bark after you say, "quiet" throw the shaker can near him or spray him with water until he stops. Make the offensive behavior less desirable by giving a consequence for it.

If you have a dog that barks all day while he is outside, work on bringing him inside. A dog left alone all day in the backyard can get bored easily and barking away the day is all that he can do.

There are also a lot more things to bark at outside than inside. Squirrels, birds and leaves blowing in the wind are all sure-fire stimulus to get any dog barking. Being separated from his family and home alone all day may be stress provoking which may also cause barking, whining and other vocalizations.

If your dog must stay outside for extended periods of time, make sure he has plenty of things to keep him busy. Leaving him with several Kongs stuffed with tasty treats should keep him busy while your away. Play ball, take him for a walk, or engage him in some other exercise before you leave. A dog that is asleep in the corner is not barking or digging or chewing for that matter. Proper exercise is fundamental if you truly want to stop many annoying canine habits. Don't underestimate it. Doggie day care is another great option to keep in mind.

Owner activated anti-bark devices such as the spray bottle and shaker can are often very effective. In addition there are some devices that can be used when barking occurs in the owner's absence. The ABS collar painlessly emits a spray of citronella each time the dog barks. Most dogs find the smell and noise unpleasant. When used in conjunction with a behavior modification program this device is usually sufficient to serve as a consistent deterrent to uncontrollable barking in the owner's absence.

If punishment alone is used dogs may become "collar-wise". They will learn they cannot bark with the collar on, but when it is off the barking will return. Our focus is always on teaching the correct behavior rather than just reacting to bad behavior. Set your dog and yourself up to succeed.

Chapter 11
Reliable Recalls

Does your dog run the other way when you call him? Does he have "selective hearing" when you call his name? A few simple changes in *your* behavior can get your dog racing to you – every time. Come is probably the most important command your dog can learn. It doesn't matter how great he does anything else if you can't get him out of the street and back to you where it is safe. If you only have a little time to train, this is the command you should work on. Get in the habit of periodically asking your dog just to come check in with you throughout the day.

The first step is to start small. Don't take your dog to the park where there are a million distractions and then become frustrated when he ignores your calls. Set yourself up for success. Start in an area with few distractions and have him come from just a foot or two away. As he gets the idea and his recalls are more consistent – then start adding distractions and distance. The further away you get the harder it is for your dog to come to you.

Take a lure, anything your dog wants (usually food but it could also be a toy or ball) to coax him to you. Say your dog's name, if he looks at you follow with the word "come". If he doesn't look at you don't bother asking him to come he's not interested in you and is not going to come. If you keep calling him when he ignores you, he will learn your commands are meaningless and continue to ignore you forever. Your dog is not deaf or stupid, he just doesn't see the point in paying attention to you.

The more you say something the less it means.

The more you say his name or "come" and he ignore you the more those commands mean nothing to him. If he is not interested in you do something that interests him. Put a treat on his nose and wiggle it towards you. As you do this say, "come" in a praise or command tone. Make him want to come to you.

As he comes to you praise him and then give him the treat when he gets to you. Even though he may only be coming from two feet away he is learning that coming to you is great. That is the first step. When he is consistently coming from two feet away, then you go three feet, then four feet, then five feet and so on. It is always a party to come to you. Never call your dog and do something negative when he comes. Do not call your dog and then put him outside, or give him a bath or yell at him. He will learn very quickly that coming is a bad thing. Dogs that do not come when called usually either have owners that over use the command until it is meaningless or they have learned coming is negative.

When your dog is getting the idea and coming to you fairly consistently, then ask him to sit before he gets the treat. So now the behavior we are looking for is "come-sit". Come should mean come, sit and wait for further instructions. It does not mean come fling yourself at me and then run away. By rewarding your dog to sit when he gets to you, he will not jump.

As your dog progresses with no distractions – add some. Take your dog in the backyard and practice the same exercise; come, sit, reward, repeat. Remember the bigger the distraction the bigger the motivator. So if you need to use a better treat to make it worth his while to come, use it. No offense, but there are a lot more interesting things other than you in the world. Your dog sees you all the time. But that snail, now that's exciting. So be more exciting than the snail or leaf or whatever has caught your dog's eye. As your dog gets better you work away from the food, but you have to start somewhere.

Also, remember your body language. Dogs are nonverbal communicators so body language is very important to them. Crouching down low is more inviting than standing up straight. Calling in a sweet tone of voice is more inviting than yelling. What would you rather come to?

As you and your dog progress you need to test your dog with bigger distractions and longer distances. However, you always need to keep your dog's safety as top priority. When working with your dog in an unfenced area always keep him on leash or use a lunge/long line. The long line is basically a long leash that comes in a variety of lengths. I personally prefer the fifteen foot length. It provides enough distance to test your dog without letting him get too far.

Come is a perfect example of how we must first teach and then test. Just because your dog does it once doesn't necessarily mean he knows the command in all circumstances. So to have a truly reliable recall you need practice with your dog in a variety of situations. No matter where you practice, however, keep the training fun and motivational. Using a variety of rewards helps to keep your dog interested.

Chapter 12
Exercise

A tired dog is a happy owner.

You must actively exercise your dog several
times a day. Research your dog's breed.
What he was selectively bred for will not only tell
you how much exercise he may need but also the
best way to do it. A herding dog, that was bred to
run all day in the field chasing sheep has loads of
energy that needs to be expended - every day. My
many years of working with dogs has taught me that
most behavior problems are symptomatic of dogs
simply not getting enough exercise. They get into
trouble when they get bored. Your mantra to
remember as you live with a dog, especially a
working dog, is *a tired dog is a happy owner.*

A dog that is sleeping peacefully in his bed is not
chewing your shoes, redecorating the landscaping or
barking at the neighbors. A tired dog is a beautiful
thing. So how do you achieve this nirvana? Engage
your dog in play. If you have a water dog get him a
plastic kiddy pool. Throw some ice cubes or treats
into the water. It's very entertaining to watch.
Use your dog's natural instincts to guide your play.

A terrier is hard-wired to dig. They were bred to hunt vermin. Digging comes naturally to them so use it. For terriers don't fill the kiddy pool with water, fill it with sand or dirt. Burying treats and toys and encourage him to search for them. Cheer him on as he finds the buried treasure. This will not necessarily teach him to dig elsewhere. In fact it may discourage digging in other areas of your yard because he finds all the really good stuff is his digging pit. Years of selective breeding have given him a strong desire to dig, your job is to direct that desire into some positive activity. Oh, and don't let the diminutive size of some terriers fool you, they are no lap dog.

Fetch is my personal favorite dog sport. I love it because I can rest while my dogs do all the work. You can play fetch with your dog while you are watching t.v., surfing the net or reading a book. It is the most versatile game ever. If you live in a two story house throw the ball up the stairs to make him work even harder for it. A few minutes of fetch are easy to incorporate into your lifestyle and are so important to your dog.

To get your dog to fetch, encourage it. Throw the ball and praise him like crazy as he chases after it. He probably won't bring it back the first few times, unless he is of the retriever persuasion. That's o.k., just throw another ball and cheer him on for chasing that one. The first step is chasing after the ball.

The second step is actually bringing it back. I can almost guarantee we won't bring it all the way back to you the first few times or so. Learning is a progression. He's not going to be fantastic at it until he's learned it. But he will get better and better the more you encourage it.

The last step to fetch is actually releasing the ball to you. This is usually the trickiest. Don't pull the ball out of his mouth, this may encourage him to play tug-of-war instead of fetch. Either wait for him to drop the ball on his own and then pick it up and throw it again. Or, you can swap him something better for it. Show him another ball or toy or treat. After he spits out the ball, pick it up and throw it again. Continuing the game is very rewarding to him. Say a command like "drop" or "give" as you make the swap so he will learn to drop it on cue.

Swapping works great for toddlers too. Instead of prying their mouth open to get that marble out just show them a piece of candy. That marble will hit the floor faster than you can say, "thank you very much."

Of course taking your dog on walks is another great way to exercise him. To give your dog an extra workout on walks, try having him wear a doggie back pack or saddle bag. Not only does he burn off some extra energy carrying the extra weight, can also carry his own doggie bags and water.

It doesn't matter what type of exercise fits best with your dog and your schedule, just do it. Your goal is to get your dog worn out as much as you can throughout the day. As with everything else, always keep safety in mind. Dogs do not have sweat glands. They cool off by panting and drinking water. Exercise your dog when it is cool and always have fresh water for him. The pads on his feet will burn, so keep him off hot pavement.

Whatever activity you chose, you and your dog will both benefit from the exercise and the increased bonding. Now get out there and play and have fun with your dog. Always remember – a tired dog is a happy owner.

A sleepy Bosley

Chapter 13
Socialization

An important, but often overlooked, aspect of dog training is socialization. The more positive exposure your dog has to a variety of stimulus the more relaxed he will be in a variety of situations. In short, the more your dog is able to go out and experience the world the less a big deal it will be to him.

Taking an under-socialized dog to the pet store can be like taking a five year old child to Disneyland for the first time. Everything is new and exciting and they want to see it all – now. By the tenth trip to Disneyland, however, it has lost some of it's newness and is not quite so exciting.

Make a point of taking your dog on shopping trips to the pet stores and feed stores. Any place that will allow you to bring a dog inside should be on your list for visiting. The more your dog sees all the wonders that are there the less they will seem so wondrous.

Coffee places like Starbucks are one of my favorite training locations. There's usually lots of people coming and going, plenty of outdoor seating and coffee (reward yourself being a good dog owner). Bring a good chew bone or stuffed Kong for your dog and you both get a treat. These excursions are invaluable to your dog's overall development.

What you end up with is a well-adjusted, well behaved dog that you can take with you anywhere. Imagine being able to travel with your dog let alone take him shopping with you. Of course don't forget just taking your dog to the vet occasionally to teach him how to behave in the waiting room. Five minutes on a Saturday morning can make a huge impact if done properly. Again, bring a stuffed Kong and some treats. I guarantee everyone will want to meet and treat your puppy.

The more people who feed your dog the more he will love people. Having fun, treat laden visits to the vet will make it a positive experience. The last thing you want is a dog that hates the vet's office. Dogs, as do people, become afraid of what they don't know.

Fear leads to aggression. It is difficult if not impossible for your dog to receive the best health care if he bites. The sad fact is that a biting dog does not have a very long life expectancy. Aggression is generally a fatal affliction that must be prevented. Positive interaction and association with many people in many places is the answer. The Zen Chien

As important as socialization is, however, we always need to put safety first. If your puppy has not had all of his shots do not put him on the ground, especially at your vet's office. But you most certainly can hold him. Puppy preschool classes should be done in a clean safe place with only healthy puppies. Properly run classes should be mandatory for every puppy. Always use your common sense when socializing puppies.

Chapter 14
Top Ten Training Tips

1.   Socialization

Have your dog meet as many new people as possible. Socialization is vital to the healthy development of your dog. Introduce your puppy to at least twenty-one new people a week. Have new people give your dog treats for a positive association. These meetings should always be positive and in as many locations as possible to help your dog generalize. Your puppy should meet people of all different sizes, shapes, colors, with facial hair, hats, umbrellas, etc.

2.   Immunizations & Regular Exams

This is a crucially important part of your dog's health care. Discuss with your veterinarian the best ways to prevent disease. Many behavior problems stem from a physiological problem. A dog of any age can learn as long as they are healthy.

3.   Leadership

You must establish yourself and all human family

members as leaders. There are some very passive ways to achieve this; such as having your dog work for all life rewards, and have your dog wait at doorways for humans to pass first, don't walk around your dog – make *them* move. Simple commands such as sit and down are leadership exercises. Every time you ask your dog to do something and he does it, he is submitting to you. If you have children in your human pack help them to do these exercises. Having your child hold your dog's dinner dish while the dog sits for it is a very powerful leadership exercise – use it.

4.   Behavior Problems
If your dog shows some undesirable behaviors, remember to find the cause and then make a change. Lack of sufficient exercise, boredom, outside irritants/stimulus, physical or health problems as well as unintentional training can all cause unwanted behaviors to occur. Always teach what you want. Don't focus on the negative behavior; focus on a positive one. Remember to train – not complain.

5.   Consistency
Pay close attention to the words and hand signs you use. Say the correct word one time. If you say "sit, sit, sit" that is the command not "sit". Thirty minutes a day (broken up throughout the day) is your goal to work with your dog. The more you work with your dog the faster they will progress. The more consistent you are with your dog the more

consistently he will respond. The less you work with your dog, the less he will respond to you.

6. Tone of Voice
How you say something is as important as what you say. The three tones of voice are; command, reprimand, and praise. Make sure there is a distinct difference in these three types when you use them.

7. Focus On Rewards
Don't take the good behavior for granted. Always praise good behavior. Positive reinforcement is *much* more effective than punishment.

8. Variety of Rewards
Use a variety of rewards in your training. Anything your dog likes is a reward. Food, toys, attention are all great rewards – use them as such.

9. Have Fun
Use game training to turn teaching your dog new behaviors fun. Teach tricks and have relay races with friends' dogs.

10. Dog Behaviors
Dogs dig, dogs chew, dogs bark dogs urinate and defecate. These are all normal canine behaviors. They are only inappropriate when they live with us. We are the ones that made the rules; it is only fair we take time to teach the dog the rules.

Bob & Bosley

Chapter 15
Have Fun

Ideally you should spend about thirty minutes a day teaching your dog. There are no shortcuts to good behavior. The more you work with your dog—the faster he will progress.

However, you should not have training sessions longer than ten minutes. Keep it short and sweet and as much fun as possible for you and your dog. Try and incorporate games and tricks with the basics to keep it interesting. If your dog is having an off day, end the session and try again later. No need to get frustrated, just take a break.

The more you put into your dog now the better behaved your dog will be in the future. The goal is to have a friendly, well-behaved member of your family that is a pleasure to have around for many, many years to come.
Now go play with your dog!

When the spirits got ready to leave the earth they created a great fissure.
On one side was Man, on the other the spirits.
Man was no longer able to cross over to the spirit realm.
The fissure widened, and at the very last minute, Dog jumped across to stand with Man.
- Lakota Legend

Bob & Bosley

Recommended Reading

Bailey, Gwen: *The Perfect Puppy*.
Donaldson, Jean: *The Culture Clash*.
Dunbar, Ian & Bohnenkamp, Gwen: Behavior Booklets.
Dunbar, Ian: *How To Teach A New Dog Old Tricks*.
Dunbar, Ian: *Sirius Puppy Training* (video).
Fox, Michael: *Understanding Your Dog*.
Pryor, Karen: *Don't Shoot The Dog!*
Reid, Pamela: *Excel-Erated Learning!*
Tortora, Daniel: *Help! This Animal is Driving Me Crazy!*

Glossary of Terms

Command tone – telling the dog to exhibit a certain behavior in a low-key, neutral voice.

Extinction – when a behavior is not reinforced (ignored) it dies. The behavior may get worse before it dies out as the dog tries everything to get it to work before he finally gives up.

Learning – changes in behavior based on experience.

Motivator – whatever your dog finds rewarding. (toy, food treat, meal, praise, walk, companionship)

Negative reinforcement – cessation of something unpleasant at the moment of desired behavior.

Positive reinforcement – a reward (event or stimulus) that increases the probability that the response will reoccur.

Praise tone – higher pitched, baby talk, smile when praising.

Punishment – an adverse stimulus that stops a behavior. Punishment does not eliminate behavior; organisms learn how to avoid the punishment not the behavior.

Reprimand tone – lower, gruffer voice. Let dog know the behavior is incorrect.

Reward based training – simple, very efficient, low margin of error.

Surface preference – surface dog prefers to eliminate on, i.e. grass, cement, and carpet.

About the Author

Cindy & Bosley

Cindy Scott is a professional Trainer and Behavioral Consultant who has professionally trained dogs and their owners since 1993. She is the Director of Dogs Etc. where she consults with owners in private in-home sessions as well as in group classes. She received her Bachelor of Arts Degree from California State University at Fullerton and continues to work with Behaviorists and Veterinarians from around the world to stay up-to-date on the latest training techniques and learning theories.

This book is the result of the need she saw for busy people like her to incorporate the principles of effective dog training into their hectic lives.

Get the maximum amount of results with a the minimum amount of effort to achieve enlightened training and get a fabulous dog.

Cindy's website address is my-zen-dog.com. Here Cindy posts information about her products and services. You can also sign up for her monthly newsletters. For more or to schedule a speaking engagement or interview please contact Cindy at dogsetc@yahoo.com or (714)393-0432.

About the Photographer

Lisa Scarsi

Lisa Scarsi has always been passionate about animals and animal welfare. At the age of six she wrote her first letter to the President to voice her opinions on animal welfare. Her career has included; twelve years in advertising and communications,ten years of being a mom to two amazing human children, 30 plus years of parenting the many, many pets that have been her own (and some freeloaders who showed up at her door), a few years of volunteering with animal and child welfare organizations and more recently she merged a few of her passions to start her own photography studio.

She focuses her efforts on creating portraits of pets, children and horses that capture their innocence, emotion and essence. She lives in Southern California with her husband, two human children and a mini-menagerie. She often travels to create storytelling portraiture for private clients and organizations that do good for pets and people. To see more of her work go to Lisa Scarsi Photography: www.lisascarsi.com

Get The Book

For a paperback copy of this book - to give to family, friends, or as a gift.

Go to *my-zen-dog.com or Amazon.com*

WELLNESS...

It's different things to different people. A crisis exists
today. Millions of people are unwell.
Why Wellness?
Why am such a fanatic about getting and staying
well? I have 2 very important reasons. My
sons Alexander and Harrison. I know it sounds corny
and all. But I not only want to be around a long, long
time to enjoy them I also don't want to burden them
with taking care of me.

Harrison & Alexander

I'm very excited to have found a company like
Nikken that has amazing products (over 200) that are
the highest quality and make having a wellness home
simple. Having the best air, water and sleep along
with nutrition is essential to good health. It's shocking
to find out the truth behind what we think is healthy
really is not.

To Get Healthy & Make Your Home A Wellness Home

Go To
nikken.com / cindyscott

Proof

Made in the USA
Charleston, SC
15 July 2011